$\mathcal{P}$resented to: <u>Mary Jane Bergen</u>

$\mathcal{F}$rom: <u>Kally de Mato</u>

$\mathcal{D}$ate: <u>8-3-02</u>

Cherished Thoughts...

on Friendship

BOK4016

$\mathcal{W}$e have
sworn friendship
with each other
in the name
of the LORD.

—*1 Samuel 20:42*

$\mathcal{F}$ortify yourself with a flock of friends! You can select them at random, write to one, dine with one, visit one, or take your problems to one. There is always at least one who will understand, inspire, and give you the lift you need at the time.

—GEORGE MATTHEW ADAMS

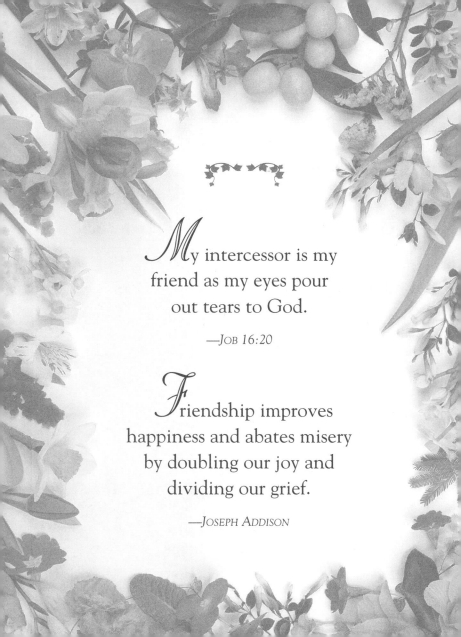

*M*y intercessor is my
friend as my eyes pour
out tears to God.

—JOB 16:20

*F*riendship improves
happiness and abates misery
by doubling our joy and
dividing our grief.

—JOSEPH ADDISON

$\mathcal{A}$ doubtful friend is
worse than a certain enemy.
Let a man be one thing or
the other, and we then know
how to meet him.

—AESOP

$\mathcal{I}$ will say,
"Peace be
within you."

—PSALM 122:8

*M*y friend will tell me my faults in private.

—ANONYMOUS

*W*ithout friends, no one would choose to live, though he had all other goods.

—ARISTOTLE

*F*riendship is the shadow of evening, it grows until the sun of life sets.

—JEAN DE LAFONTAINE

*H*ow good and pleasant it
is when brothers live together
in unity!

—*Psalm 133:1*

*T*here's a special kind of freedom
friends enjoy. Freedom to share
innermost thoughts, to show their
true feelings. The freedom to
simply be themselves.

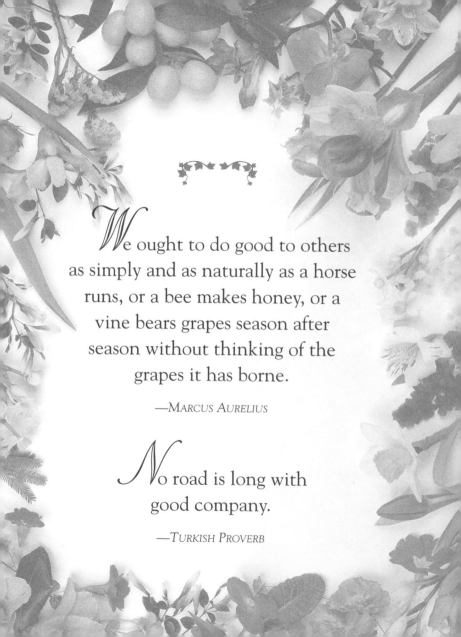

*W*e ought to do good to others
as simply and as naturally as a horse
runs, or a bee makes honey, or a
vine bears grapes season after
season without thinking of the
grapes it has borne.

—MARCUS AURELIUS

*N*o road is long with
good company.

—TURKISH PROVERB

$\mathcal{L}$et love and
faithfulness never
leave you.

—PROVERBS 3:3

What a Friend we have in Jesus,
All our sins and griefs to bear!
What a privilege to carry
Everything to God in prayer.

Can we find a friend so faithful
Who will all our sorrows share?
Jesus knows our every weakness;
Take it to the Lord in prayer.

—JOSEPH MEDLICOTT SCRIVEN

*D*o not rebuke a mocker or
he will hate you; rebuke a wise
man and he will love you.

—*Proverbs 9:8*

A true friend will not
always agree with you, but will
be true to your best interests.

—*Nicole Beale*

From quiet homes and first
beginning,
Out to the undiscovered ends,
There's nothing worth the wear
of winning,
But laughter and the love of
friends.

—HILAIRE BELLOC

$\mathcal{L}$ove covers
over all wrongs.

—PROVERBS 10:12

$\mathcal{W}$e cannot tell the precise moment when friendship is formed. As in filling a vessel drop by drop there is at last a drop which makes it run over, so in a series of kindnesses there is at last one which makes the heart run over.

—SAMUEL JOHNSON

*B*etter a meal of vegetables where there is love than a fattened calf with hatred.

—*P*ROVERBS *15:17*

*H*e whose hand is clasped in friendship cannot throw mud.

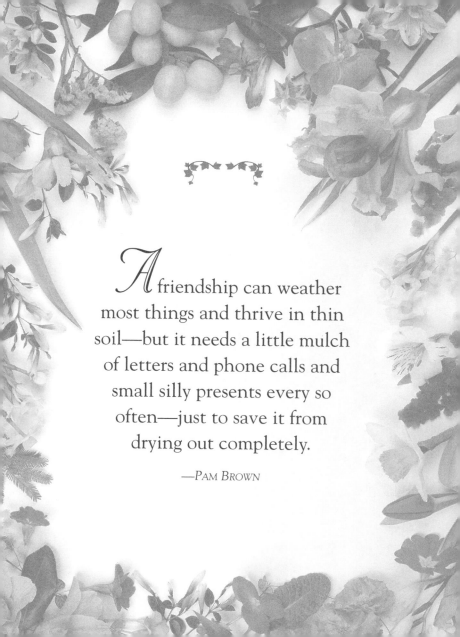

$\mathcal{A}$ friendship can weather most things and thrive in thin soil—but it needs a little mulch of letters and phone calls and small silly presents every so often—just to save it from drying out completely.

—PAM BROWN

*M*ay the LORD's
unfailing love
be my comfort.

—PSALM 119:76

*Y*ou're my friend—
What a thing friendship is,
    world without end!
How it gives the heart and soul
    a stir-up!

—ROBERT BROWNING

*E*ach bright day has its sunset
And each rainbow has its end.
But no cloud can
hide the light
Of my dear and
trusted friend.

$\mathcal{H}$e who covers over an
offense promotes love,
but whoever repeats the
matter separates close friends.

—PROVERBS 17:9

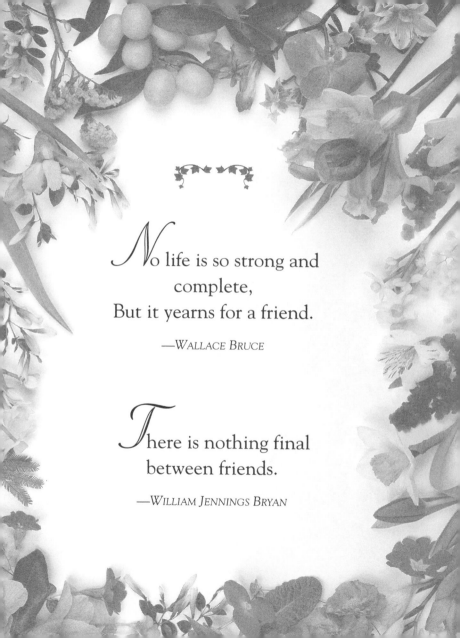

*N*o life is so strong and
complete,
But it yearns for a friend.

—Wallace Bruce

*T*here is nothing final
between friends.

—William Jennings Bryan

*T*here is a
friend who sticks
closer than a
brother.

—PROVERBS 18:24

*H*onest men esteem and value nothing so much in this world as a real friend. Such a one is as it were another self, to whom we impart our most secret thoughts, who partakes of our joy, and comforts us in our affliction; add to this, that his company is an everlasting pleasure to us.

—*PILPAY*

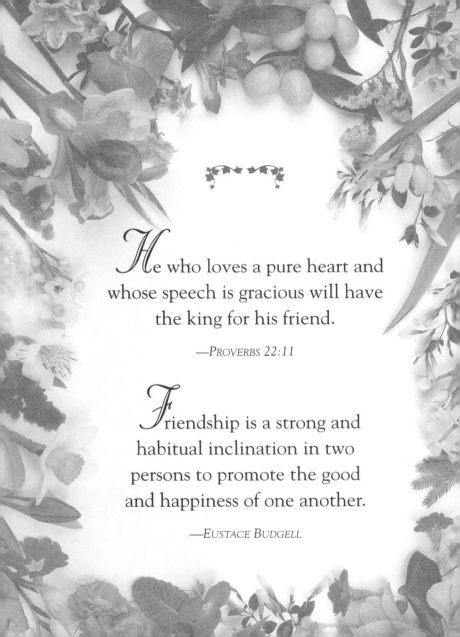

$\mathcal{H}$e who loves a pure heart and whose speech is gracious will have the king for his friend.

—PROVERBS *22:11*

$\mathcal{F}$riendship is a strong and habitual inclination in two persons to promote the good and happiness of one another.

—EUSTACE BUDGELL

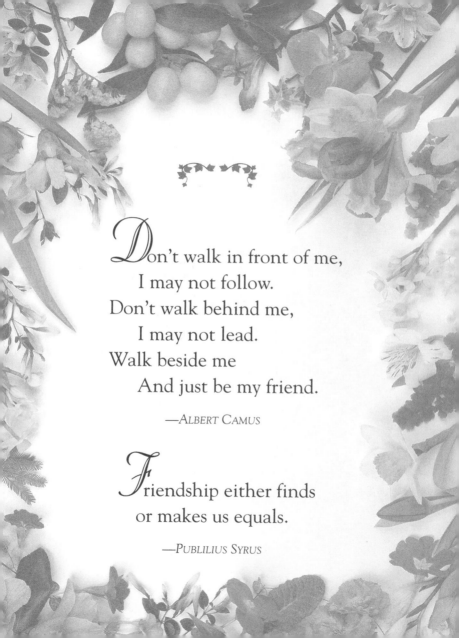

*D*on't walk in front of me,
I may not follow.
Don't walk behind me,
I may not lead.
Walk beside me
And just be my friend.

—ALBERT CAMUS

*F*riendship either finds
or makes us equals.

—PUBLILIUS SYRUS

*W*ounds from
a friend can
be trusted.

—PROVERBS 27:6

*S*mall service is true service while it lasts...
The daisy, by the shadow it casts,
Protects the lingering dewdrop from the sun.

—WILLIAM WORDSWORTH

$\mathcal{W}$e are so very rich if we
know just a few people in a way
in which we know no others.

—CATHERINE BRAMWELL-BOOTH

$\mathcal{T}$rue friendship is Love
without its wings!

—LORD BYRON

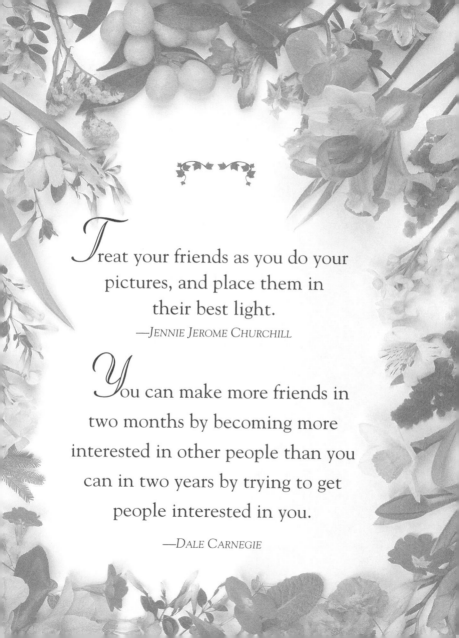

*T*reat your friends as you do your
pictures, and place them in
their best light.

—*Jennie Jerome Churchill*

*Y*ou can make more friends in
two months by becoming more
interested in other people than you
can in two years by trying to get
people interested in you.

—*Dale Carnegie*

*D*o not forsake your friend and the friend of your father.

—PROVERBS 27:10

$\mathcal{F}$riendship makes prosperity more brilliant, and lightens adversity by dividing and sharing it.

—CICERO

$\mathcal{F}$riendships are the ship the Lord often launches to keep my boat afloat.

—PATSY CLAIRMONT

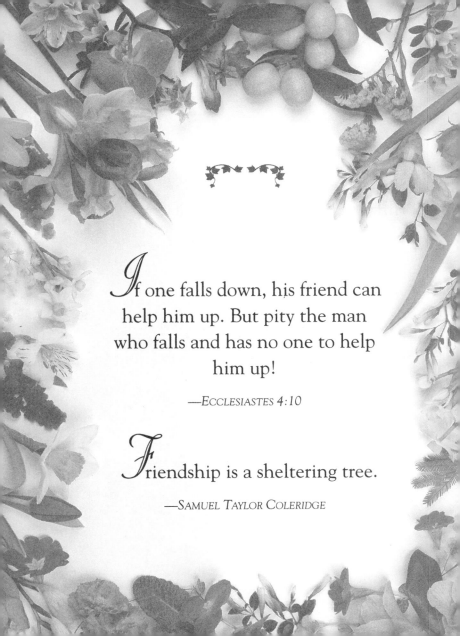

*I*f one falls down, his friend can help him up. But pity the man who falls and has no one to help him up!

—*ECCLESIASTES 4:10*

*F*riendship is a sheltering tree.

—*SAMUEL TAYLOR COLERIDGE*

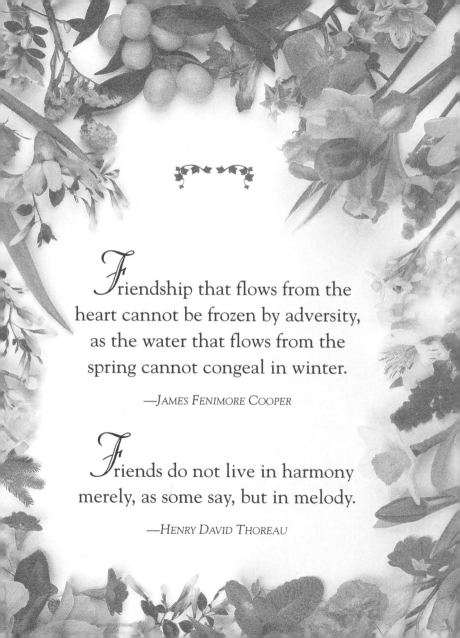

*F*riendship that flows from the
heart cannot be frozen by adversity,
as the water that flows from the
spring cannot congeal in winter.

—JAMES FENIMORE COOPER

*F*riends do not live in harmony
merely, as some say, but in melody.

—HENRY DAVID THOREAU

*A*s iron sharpens iron, so one man sharpens another.

—PROVERBS 27:17

$\mathcal{B}$e generous and understanding. Let no one come to you without feeling better and happier when they leave. Be the living expression of God's kindness: with kindness on your face...in your eyes...in your smile...in your warm greeting.

—MOTHER TERESA

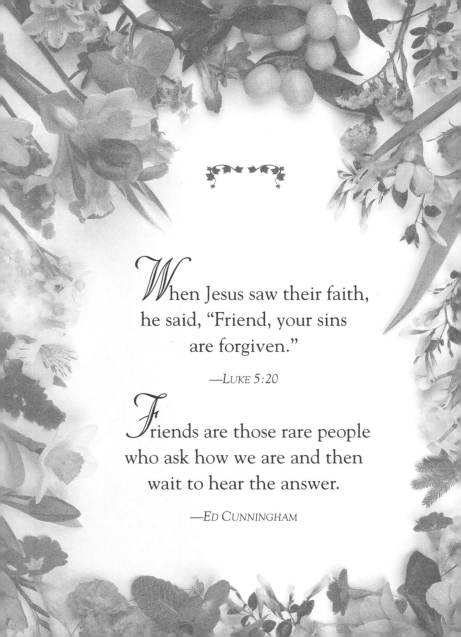

*W*hen Jesus saw their faith,
he said, "Friend, your sins
are forgiven."

—LUKE 5:20

*F*riends are those rare people
who ask how we are and then
wait to hear the answer.

—ED CUNNINGHAM

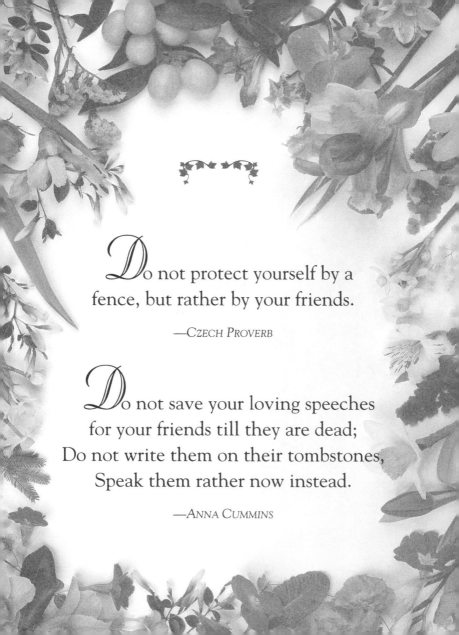

*D*o not protect yourself by a
fence, but rather by your friends.

—CZECH PROVERB

*D*o not save your loving speeches
for your friends till they are dead;
Do not write them on their tombstones,
Speak them rather now instead.

—ANNA CUMMINS

A new command I give you: Love one another.

—JOHN 13:34

*O*h, I have roamed o'er many lands,
And many friends I've met;
Not one fair scene or kindly smile
Can this fond heart forget.

—THOMAS HAYNES BAYLY

*F*riendship! mysterious cement
of the soul! Sweetener of life!
and solder of society!

—ROBERT BLAIR

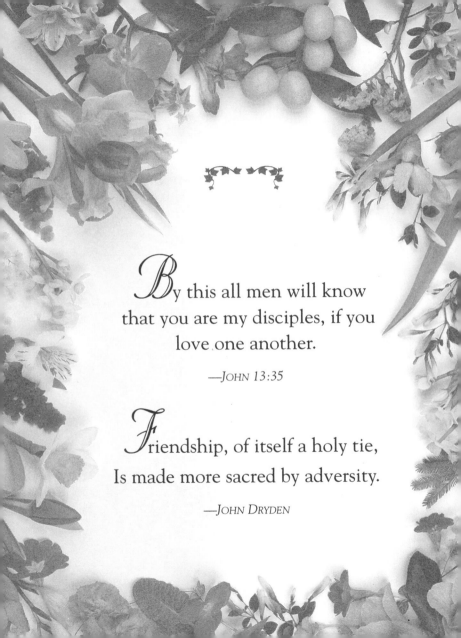

$\mathcal{B}$y this all men will know
that you are my disciples, if you
love one another.

—JOHN 13:35

$\mathcal{F}$riendship, of itself a holy tie,
Is made more sacred by adversity.

—JOHN DRYDEN

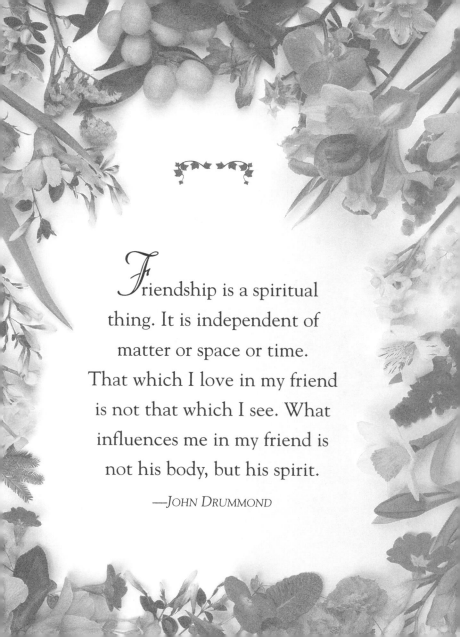

Friendship is a spiritual
thing. It is independent of
matter or space or time.
That which I love in my friend
is not that which I see. What
influences me in my friend is
not his body, but his spirit.

—JOHN DRUMMOND

$\mathcal{L}$ove each
other as I have
loved you.

—JOHN 15:12

*I*f a man does not make new acquaintances as he advances through life, he will soon find himself left alone. A man should keep his friendship in constant repair.

—SAMUEL JOHNSON

*W*e ought to remember those friends who are absent as well as those who are present.

—DIOGENES LAERTIUS

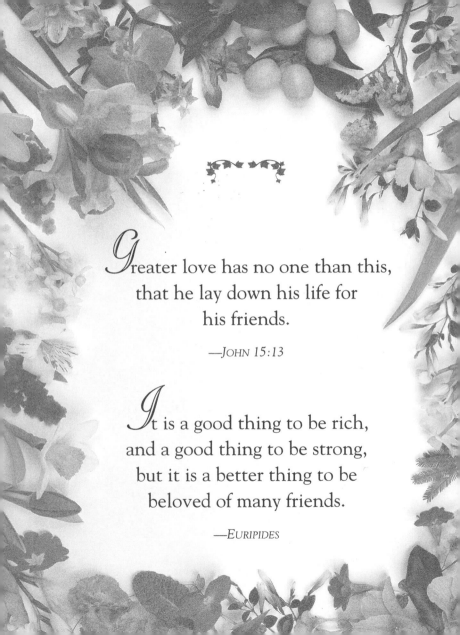

*G*reater love has no one than this,
that he lay down his life for
his friends.

—*JOHN 15:13*

*I*t is a good thing to be rich,
and a good thing to be strong,
but it is a better thing to be
beloved of many friends.

—*EURIPIDES*

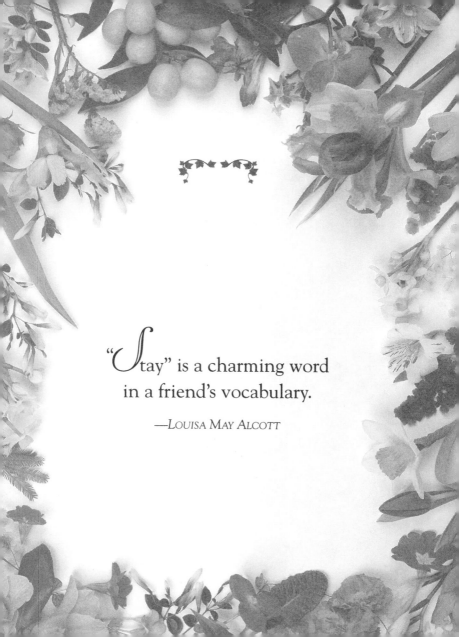

"*S*tay" is a charming word
in a friend's vocabulary.

—LOUISA MAY ALCOTT

I have called
you friends.

—*John 15:15*

$\mathcal{B}$lest be the tie that binds
Our hearts in Christian love;
The fellowship of kindred minds,
Is like to that above.

—JOHN FAWCETT

$\mathcal{W}$e have been friends together
In sunshine and in shade.

—CAROLINE E. S. NORTON

$\mathcal{B}$e devoted to one another in
brotherly love. Honor one another
above yourselves.

—*ROMANS 12:10*

$\mathcal{M}$y best friend is the one who
brings out the best in me.

—*HENRY FORD*

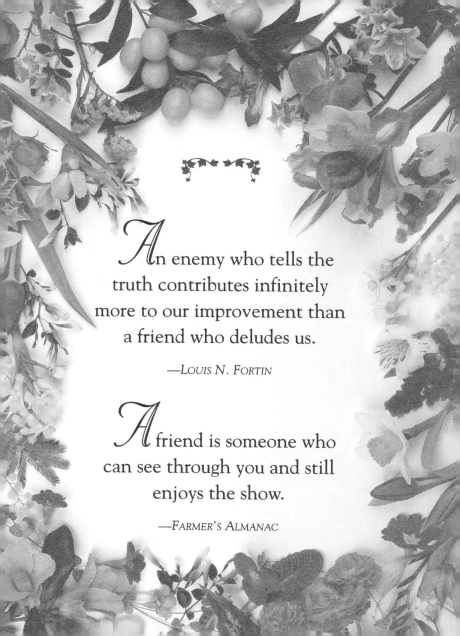

$\mathcal{A}$n enemy who tells the
truth contributes infinitely
more to our improvement than
a friend who deludes us.

—LOUIS N. FORTIN

$\mathcal{A}$ friend is someone who
can see through you and still
enjoys the show.

—FARMER'S ALMANAC

*R*ejoice with those who rejoice; mourn with those who mourn.

—ROMANS 12:15

*N*o man is the whole of himself;
his friends are the rest of him.

—*HARRY EMERSON FOSDICK*

*B*e slow in choosing a friend, slower
in changing.

—*BENJAMIN FRANKLIN*

*T*he man who treasures his friends
is usually solid
gold himself.

—*MARJORIE HOLMES*

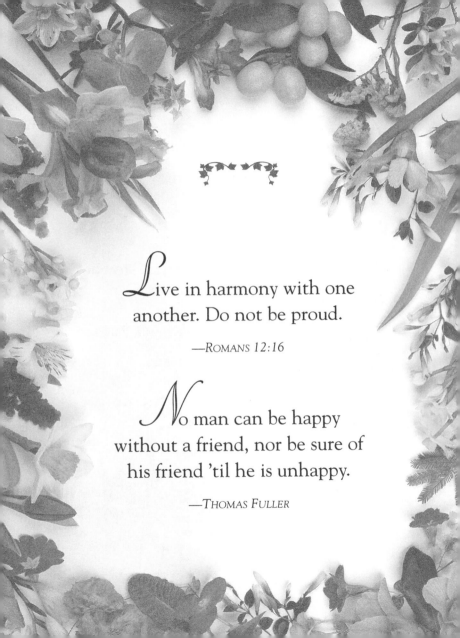

*L*ive in harmony with one
another. Do not be proud.

—*Romans 12:16*

*N*o man can be happy
without a friend, nor be sure of
his friend 'til he is unhappy.

—*Thomas Fuller*

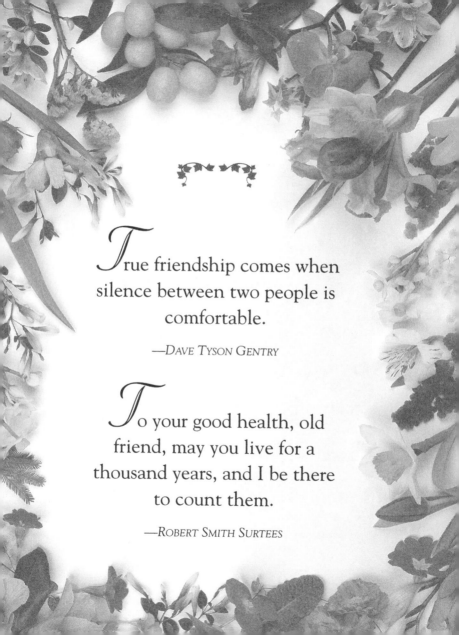

*T*rue friendship comes when silence between two people is comfortable.

—DAVE TYSON GENTRY

*T*o your good health, old friend, may you live for a thousand years, and I be there to count them.

—ROBERT SMITH SURTEES

$\mathcal{B}$e careful
to do what is right
in the eyes
of everybody.

—ROMANS 12:17

*F*riendship is not a fruit for enjoyment only, but also an opportunity for service.

—*GREEK PROVERB*

*T*he making of friends, who are real friends, is the best token we have of success in life.

—*EDWARD EVERETT HALE*

*I*f it is possible, as far as it depends on you, live at peace with everyone.

—*ROMANS 12:18*

$\mathcal{F}$riends are the sunshine of life.

—JOHN HAY

$\mathcal{I}$ want a sofa, as I want a friend,
upon which I can repose
familiarly.

—WILLIAM MAKEPEACE THACKERY

$\mathcal{T}$he best mirror is an old friend.

—GEORGE HERBERT

$\mathcal{F}$riendship needs no words—
it is solitude delivered from the
anguish of loneliness.

—DAG HAMMARSKJÖLD

Love . . .
**rejoices
with the truth.**

—1 CORINTHIANS 13:6

The beauty of a friend is only a taste of what God is. It should be seen as an image of God, an enticement towards him. If the two spend their lives trying to look at each other only, they will never be open to the absolute fullness in God of which this friend is only a taste.

—PAUL HINNEBUSCH

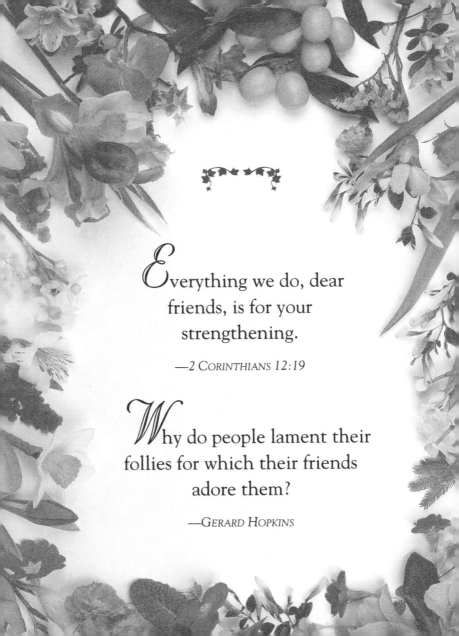

*E*verything we do, dear friends, is for your strengthening.

—*2 Corinthians 12:19*

*W*hy do people lament their follies for which their friends adore them?

—*Gerard Hopkins*

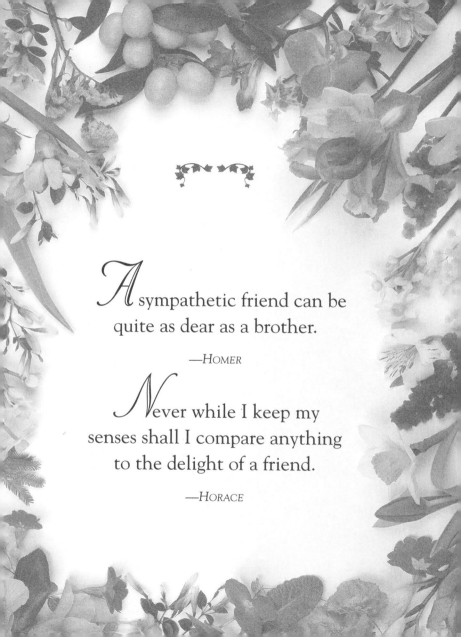

$\mathcal{A}$ sympathetic friend can be quite as dear as a brother.

—HOMER

$\mathcal{N}$ever while I keep my senses shall I compare anything to the delight of a friend.

—HORACE

*S*erve one

another

in love.

—GALATIANS 5:13

$\mathcal{A}$ true friend gives freely, advises justly, assists readily, adventures boldly, takes all patiently, defends courageously, and continues a friend unchangeable.

—WILLIAM PENN

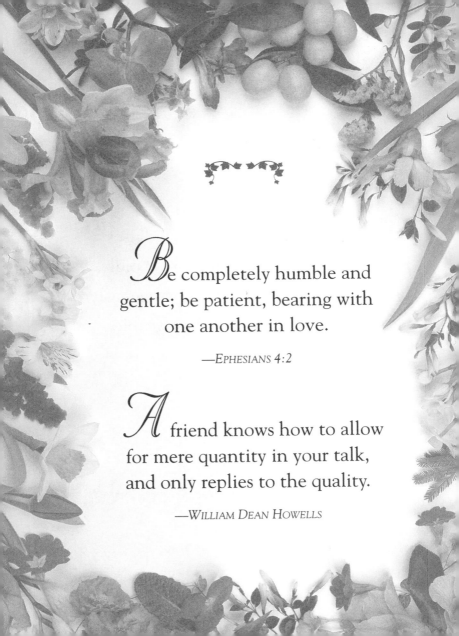

$\mathcal{B}$e completely humble and gentle; be patient, bearing with one another in love.

—EPHESIANS 4:2

$\mathcal{A}$ friend knows how to allow for mere quantity in your talk, and only replies to the quality.

—WILLIAM DEAN HOWELLS

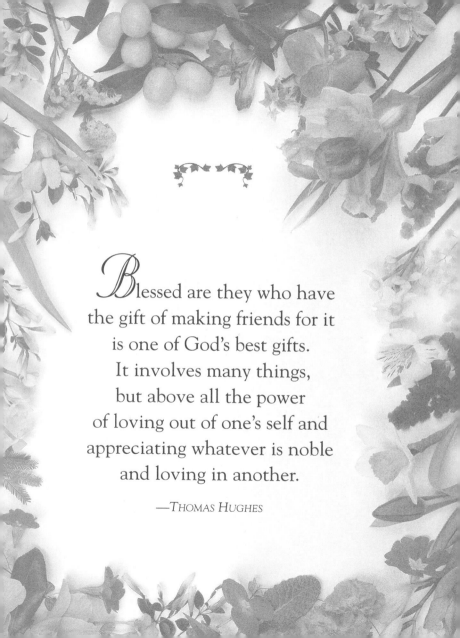

$\mathcal{B}$lessed are they who have
the gift of making friends for it
is one of God's best gifts.
It involves many things,
but above all the power
of loving out of one's self and
appreciating whatever is noble
and loving in another.

—THOMAS HUGHES

$\mathcal{B}$e kind and compassionate to one another, forgiving each other.

—*EPHESIANS 4:32*

The joy of being friends is just
A simple code of faith and trust,
A homey comradeship that stays
The threatened fear of darker days;
The kind of faith that brings to light
The good, the beautiful, and the bright;
And best and blest, and true and rare—
Is having friends who love and care!

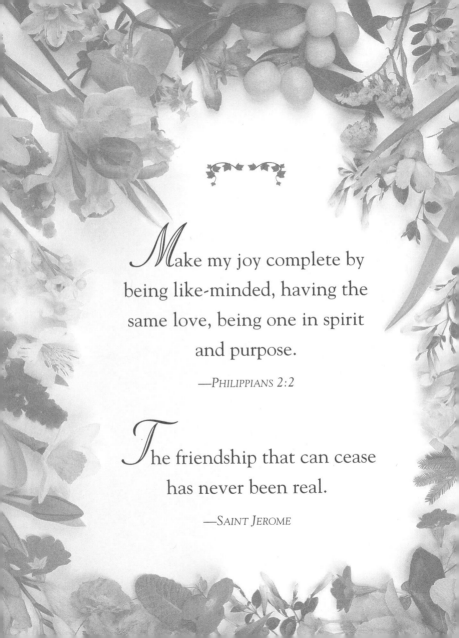

Make my joy complete by being like-minded, having the same love, being one in spirit and purpose.

—PHILIPPIANS 2:2

The friendship that can cease has never been real.

—SAINT JEROME

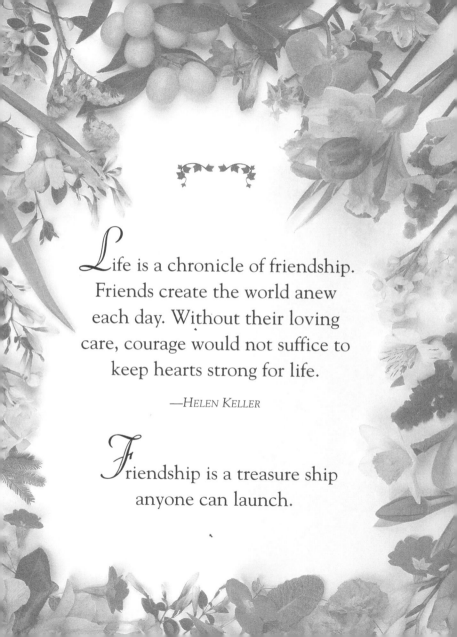

$\mathcal{L}$ife is a chronicle of friendship.
Friends create the world anew
each day. Without their loving
care, courage would not suffice to
keep hearts strong for life.

—HELEN KELLER

$\mathcal{F}$riendship is a treasure ship
anyone can launch.

You should
stand firm
in the Lord,
dear friends!

—*PHILIPPIANS 4:1*

$\mathcal{T}$rue friends don't spend time gazing into each other's eyes. They may show great tenderness toward each other, but they face in the same direction—toward common projects, interests, goals— above all, toward a common Lord.

—C. S. *Lewis*

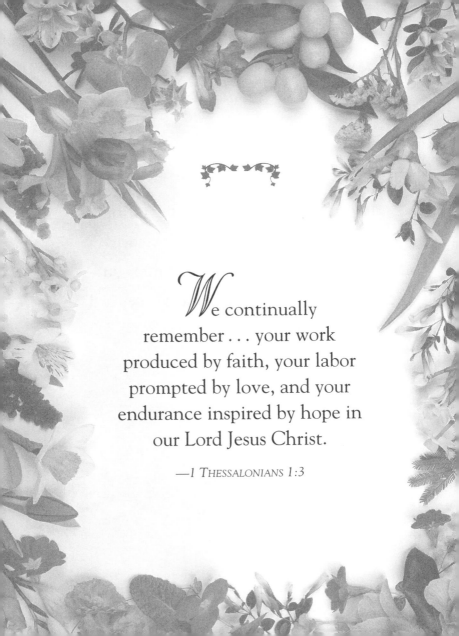

$\mathcal{W}$e continually remember . . . your work produced by faith, your labor prompted by love, and your endurance inspired by hope in our Lord Jesus Christ.

—*1 Thessalonians 1:3*

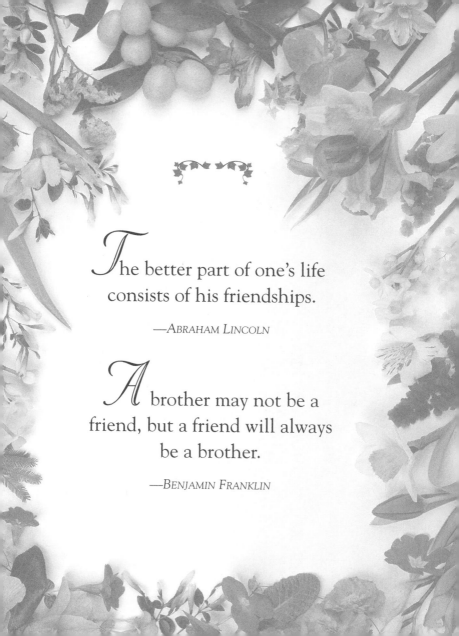

*T*he better part of one's life
consists of his friendships.

—*ABRAHAM LINCOLN*

A brother may not be a
friend, but a friend will always
be a brother.

—*BENJAMIN FRANKLIN*

*M*ay the
Lord make
your love
increase and
overflow.

—*1 Thessalonians 3:12*

I know I've never told you
In the hurried rush of days
How much your friendship helps me
In a thousand little ways;
But you've played such a part
In all I do or try to be,
I want to tell you thank you
For being friends with me.

—ANONYMOUS

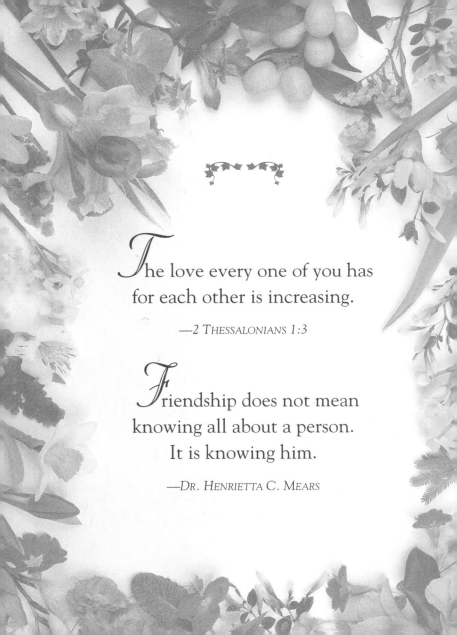

The love every one of you has
for each other is increasing.

—*2 Thessalonians 1:3*

Friendship does not mean
knowing all about a person.
It is knowing him.

—*Dr. Henrietta C. Mears*

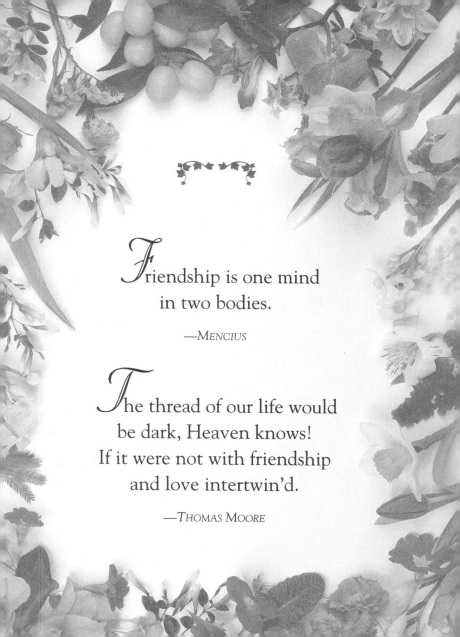

$\mathcal{F}$riendship is one mind
in two bodies.

—MENCIUS

$\mathcal{T}$he thread of our life would
be dark, Heaven knows!
If it were not with friendship
and love intertwin'd.

—THOMAS MOORE

$\mathcal{L}$ive in peace
with each other.

—1 THESSALONIANS 5:13

Abraham Lincoln was once taken to task by an associate for his attitude toward his enemies: "Why do you try to make friends of them? You should try to destroy them."

Lincoln replied gently, "Am I not destroying my enemies when I make them my friends?"

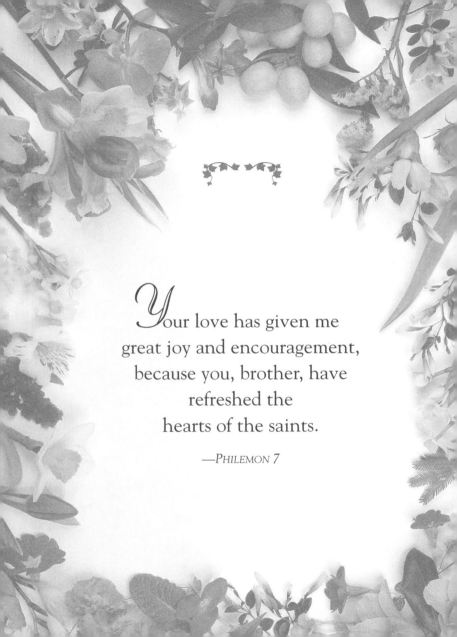

$\mathcal{Y}$our love has given me
great joy and encouragement,
because you, brother, have
refreshed the
hearts of the saints.

—*PHILEMON 7*

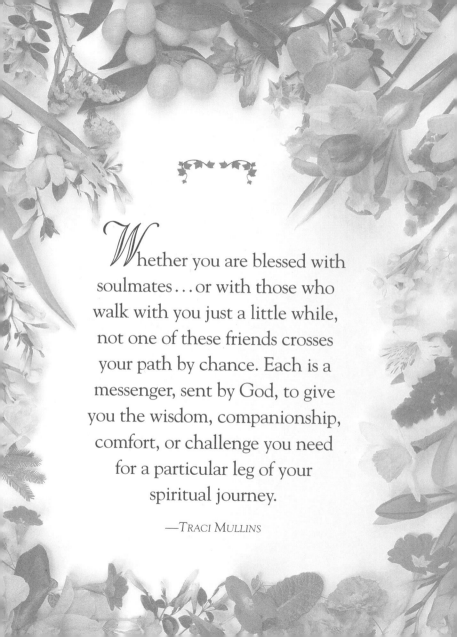

*W*hether you are blessed with soulmates...or with those who walk with you just a little while, not one of these friends crosses your path by chance. Each is a messenger, sent by God, to give you the wisdom, companionship, comfort, or challenge you need for a particular leg of your spiritual journey.

—*Traci Mullins*

$\mathcal{L}$et us
consider
how we may spur
one another on
toward love and
good deeds.

—HEBREWS 10:24

$\mathscr{I}$ never considered a difference of opinion in politics, in religion, in philosophy, as cause for withdrawing from a friend.

—THOMAS JEFFERSON

$\mathscr{D}$o good to thy friend to keep him, to thy enemy to gain him.

—BENJAMIN FRANKLIN

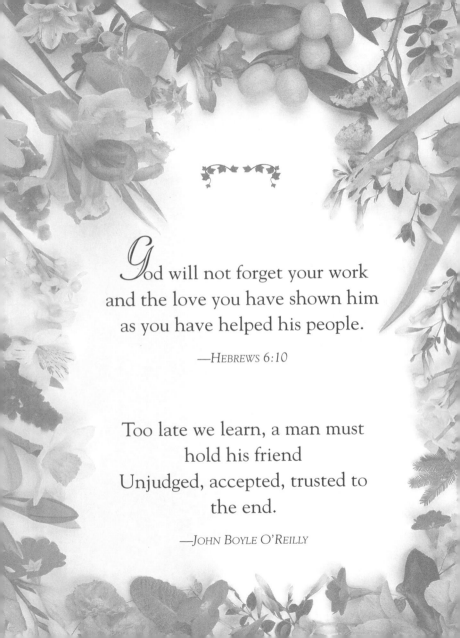

$\mathcal{G}$od will not forget your work
and the love you have shown him
as you have helped his people.

—*HEBREWS 6:10*

Too late we learn, a man must
hold his friend
Unjudged, accepted, trusted to
the end.

—*JOHN BOYLE O'REILLY*

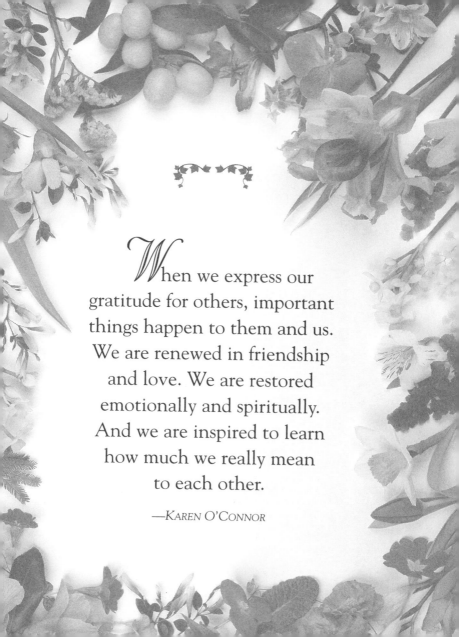

When we express our gratitude for others, important things happen to them and us. We are renewed in friendship and love. We are restored emotionally and spiritually. And we are inspired to learn how much we really mean to each other.

—KAREN O'CONNOR

*L*et us
encourage one
another.

—*HEBREWS 10:25*

$\mathcal{L}$ord, make me an instrument of Your peace. Where there is hatred let me sow love; where there is injury, pardon; where there is doubt, faith; where there is despair, hope; where there is darkness, light; and where there is sadness, joy.

—SAINT FRANCIS OF ASSISI

$\mathcal{L}$ove one another deeply,
from the heart.

—1 PETER 1:22

$\mathcal{F}$riends have all things
in common.

—PLATO

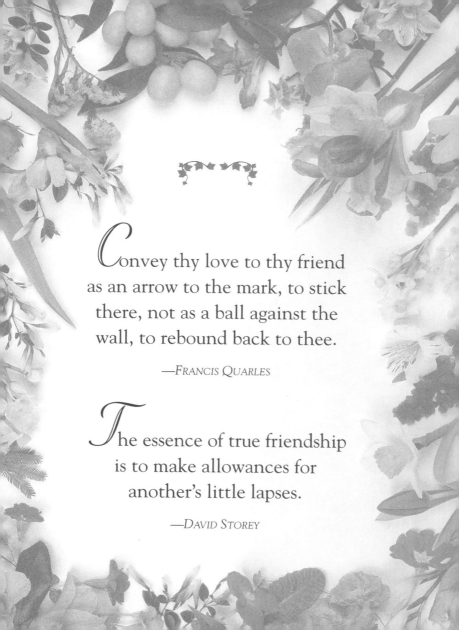

*C*onvey thy love to thy friend
as an arrow to the mark, to stick
there, not as a ball against the
wall, to rebound back to thee.

—*FRANCIS QUARLES*

*T*he essence of true friendship
is to make allowances for
another's little lapses.

—*DAVID STOREY*

$\mathcal{L}$ove the
brotherhood of
believers.

—1 PETER 2:17

*F*riendship with oneself is all-important because without it one cannot be friends with anyone else in the world.

—ELEANOR ROOSEVELT

A pleasant word is a bright ray of sunshine on a saddened heart. Therefore, give others the sunshine, and tell Jesus the rest.

—L.B. COWMAN

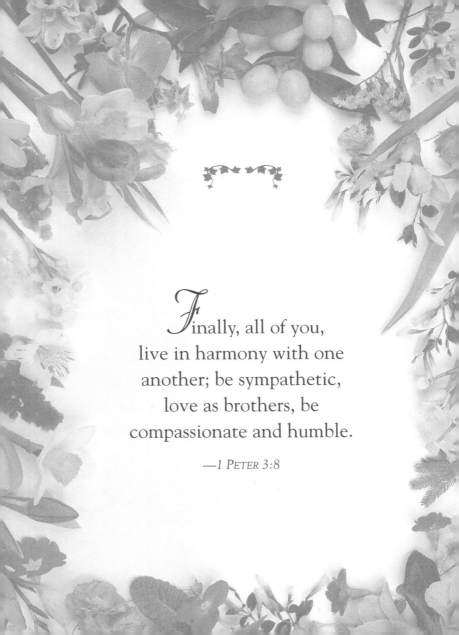

$\mathcal{F}$inally, all of you,
live in harmony with one
another; be sympathetic,
love as brothers, be
compassionate and humble.

—1 PETER 3:8

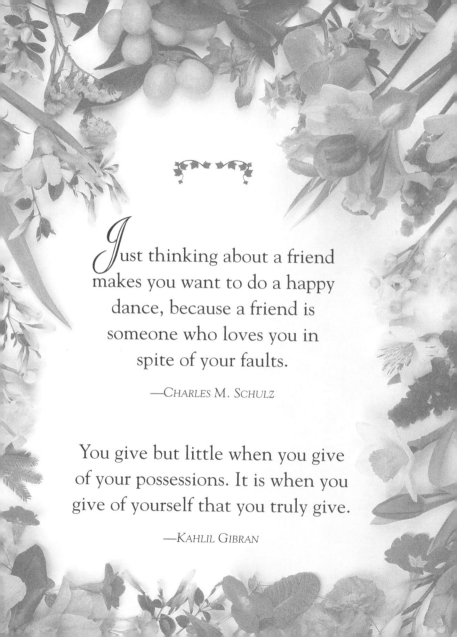

*J*ust thinking about a friend
makes you want to do a happy
dance, because a friend is
someone who loves you in
spite of your faults.

—CHARLES M. SCHULZ

You give but little when you give
of your possessions. It is when you
give of yourself that you truly give.

—KAHLIL GIBRAN

$\mathcal{L}$ove covers
over a multitude
of sins.

—1 PETER 4:8

*O*f all the gifts that a wise providence grants us to make life full and happy, friendship is the most beautiful.

—*Epicurus*

*T*he best antique is an old friend.

*O*ne can do without people, but one has need of a friend.

—*Chinese wisdom*

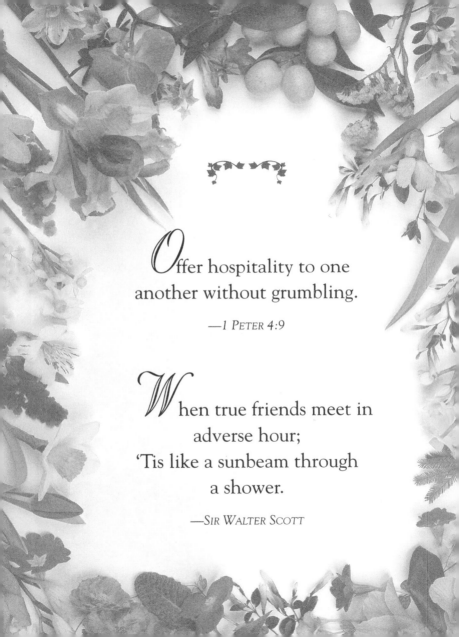

*O*ffer hospitality to one
another without grumbling.

—*1 Peter 4:9*

*W*hen true friends meet in
adverse hour;
'Tis like a sunbeam through
a shower.

—*Sir Walter Scott*

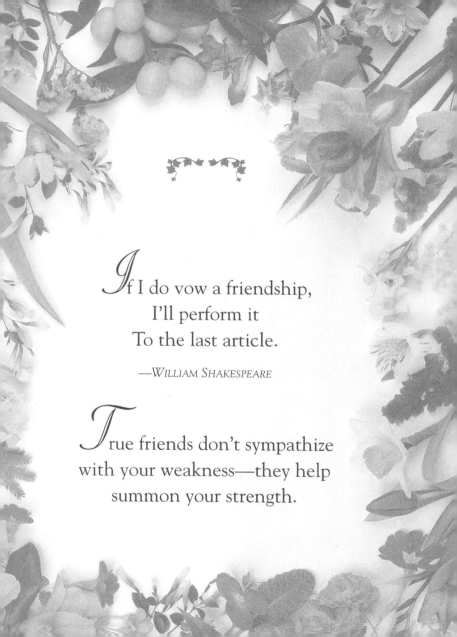

*I*f I do vow a friendship,
I'll perform it
To the last article.

—WILLIAM SHAKESPEARE

*T*rue friends don't sympathize
with your weakness—they help
summon your strength.

$\mathcal{L}$et us not love
with words . . .
but with actions
and in truth.

—1 JOHN 3:18

$\mathcal{T}$he things we do today—sowing seeds, or sharing simple truths of Christ—people will someday refer to as the first things that prompted them to think of Him.

—GEORGE MATHESON

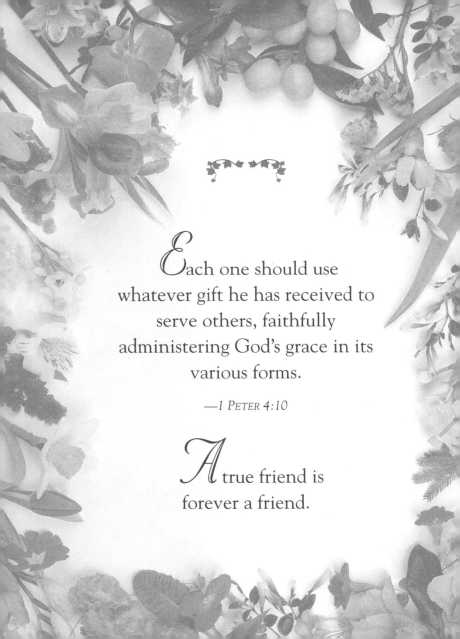

$\mathscr{E}$ach one should use whatever gift he has received to serve others, faithfully administering God's grace in its various forms.

—1 PETER 4:10

$\mathscr{A}$ true friend is forever a friend.

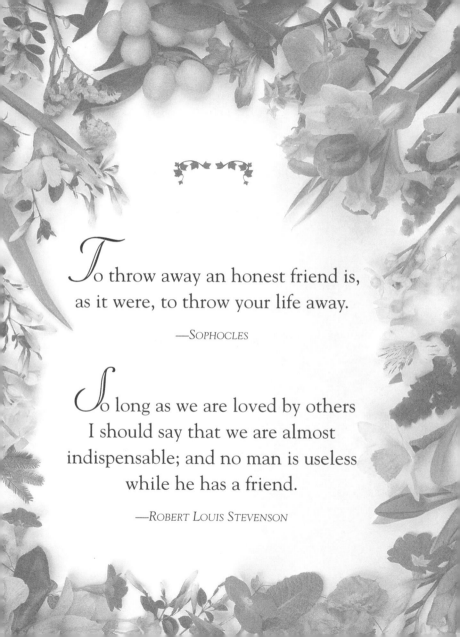

*T*o throw away an honest friend is,
as it were, to throw your life away.

—SOPHOCLES

*S*o long as we are loved by others
I should say that we are almost
indispensable; and no man is useless
while he has a friend.

—ROBERT LOUIS STEVENSON

$\mathscr{E}$veryone who loves has been born of God and knows God.

—1 JOHN 4:7

$\mathcal{H}$aving friends around for a pleasant evening is one of life's most cherished joys as far as I am concerned. But when those with me are fellow believers how much greater that joy is, for we know that it will be rekindled, one day, in eternity.

—JAMES STEWART

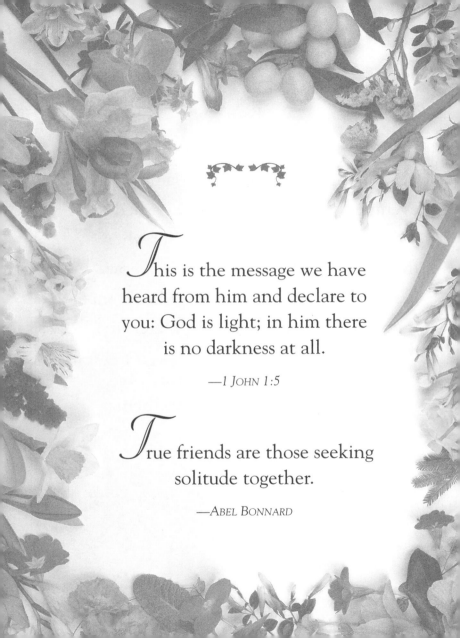

This is the message we have heard from him and declare to you: God is light; in him there is no darkness at all.

—1 John 1:5

True friends are those seeking solitude together.

—Abel Bonnard

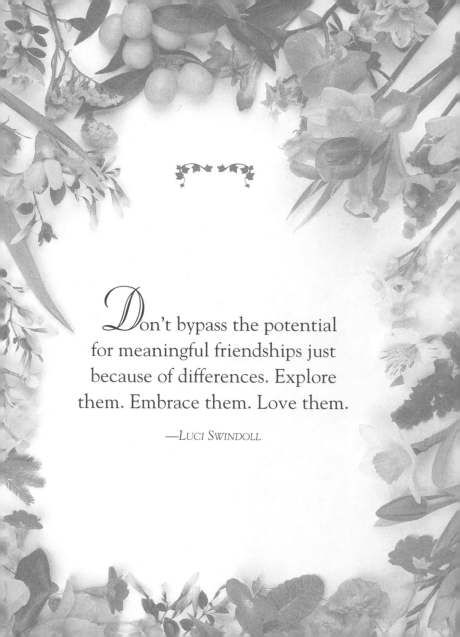

$\mathcal{D}$on't bypass the potential for meaningful friendships just because of differences. Explore them. Embrace them. Love them.

—*Luci Swindoll*

I pray that you
may enjoy good
health and that all
may go well
with you.

—*3 John 2*

*P*leasurable things give delight and satisfaction to the soul. Pleasure is found lying under an oak tree, with the cool grass beneath and the rustle of leaves above. Pleasure is sitting by a cheery fire, curled up on the couch with your favorite blanket and cup of tea. Pleasure is captured in the soft smile and gentle eyes of the one you love.

*L*ove comes from God.

—1 John 4:7

*B*y friendship you mean the greatest love, the greatest usefulness, the most noble sufferings, the severest truth, the heartiest counsel, and the greatest union of minds of which brave men and women are capable.

—Jeremy Taylor

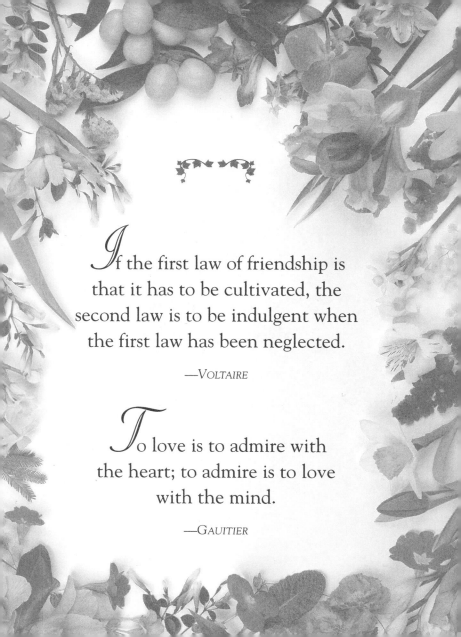

*I*f the first law of friendship is
that it has to be cultivated, the
second law is to be indulgent when
the first law has been neglected.

—VOLTAIRE

*T*o love is to admire with
the heart; to admire is to love
with the mind.

—GAUITIER

*S*ince God
so loved us, we
also ought to love
one another.

—*1 John 4:11*

$\mathcal{O}$ne recipe for friendship is the right mixture of commonality and difference. You've got to have enough in common so that you understand each other and enough difference so that there is something to exchange.

—ROBERT WEISS

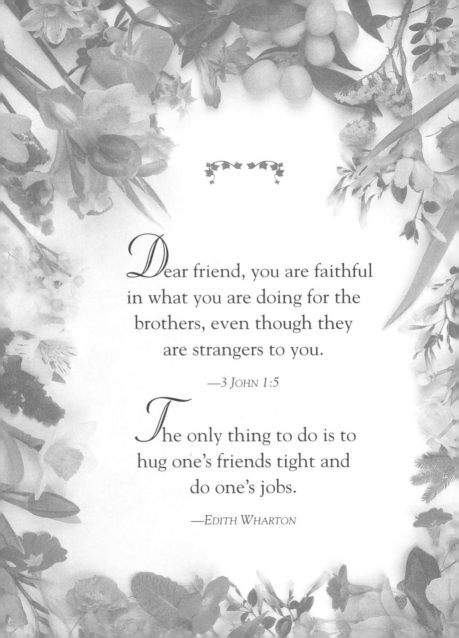

$\mathcal{D}$ear friend, you are faithful in what you are doing for the brothers, even though they are strangers to you.

—3 JOHN 1:5

$\mathcal{T}$he only thing to do is to hug one's friends tight and do one's jobs.

—EDITH WHARTON

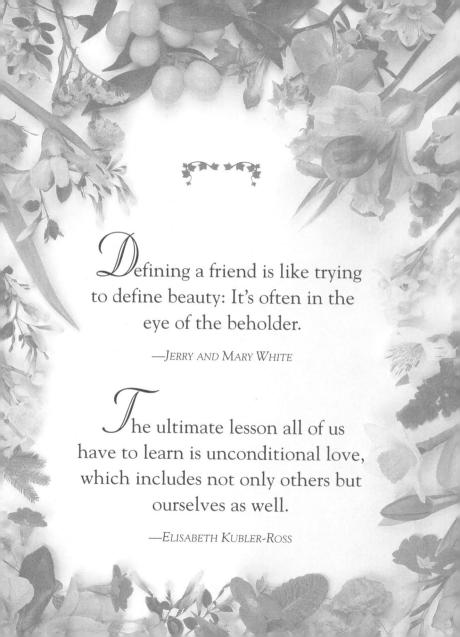

*D*efining a friend is like trying
to define beauty: It's often in the
eye of the beholder.

—*Jerry and Mary White*

*T*he ultimate lesson all of us
have to learn is unconditional love,
which includes not only others but
ourselves as well.

—*Elisabeth Kubler-Ross*

*Mercy, peace
and love be yours
in abundance.*

—JUDE 2

*F*riendship is a chain of gold
Shaped in God's all perfect mold.
Each link a smile, a laugh, a tear,
A grip of the hand, a word of cheer.
Steadfast as the ages roll
Binding closer soul to soul;
No matter how far or heavy the load
Sweet is the journey on friendship's road.

—*AUTHOR UNKNOWN*

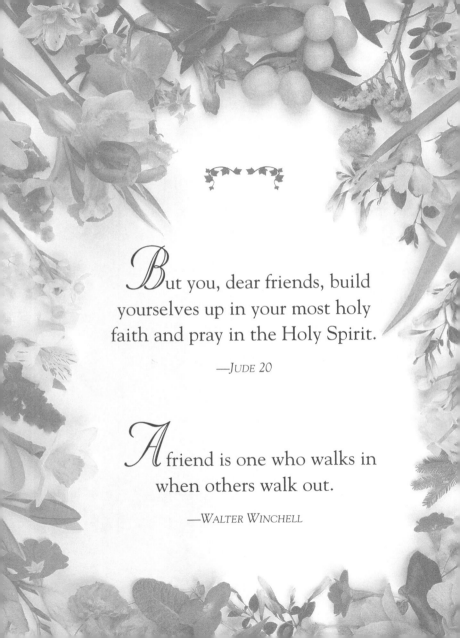

$\mathcal{B}$ut you, dear friends, build
yourselves up in your most holy
faith and pray in the Holy Spirit.

—JUDE 20

$\mathcal{A}$ friend is one who walks in
when others walk out.

—WALTER WINCHELL

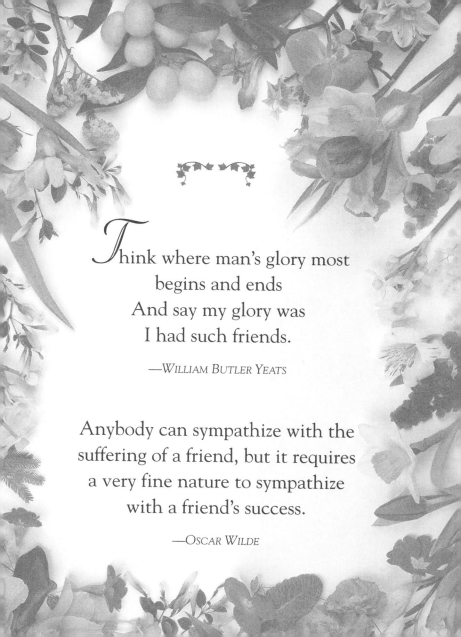

*T*hink where man's glory most
begins and ends
And say my glory was
I had such friends.

—WILLIAM BUTLER YEATS

Anybody can sympathize with the
suffering of a friend, but it requires
a very fine nature to sympathize
with a friend's success.

—OSCAR WILDE

$\mathcal{I}$am a friend
to all who fear
the LORD, to all
who follow
[his] precepts.

—PSALM 119:63

*T*he Christian should never complain
of his hard fortune while he knows that
Christ is his friend.

—*Anonymous*

A true friend is the gift of God, and
only he who made hearts can unite them.

—*Robert South*

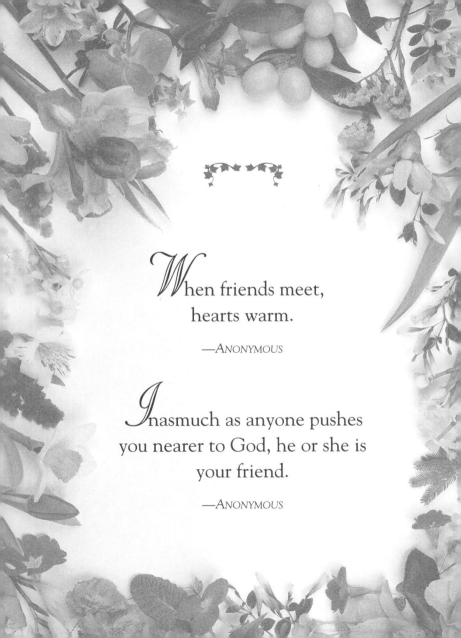

When friends meet,
hearts warm.

—*ANONYMOUS*

Inasmuch as anyone pushes
you nearer to God, he or she is
your friend.

—*ANONYMOUS*

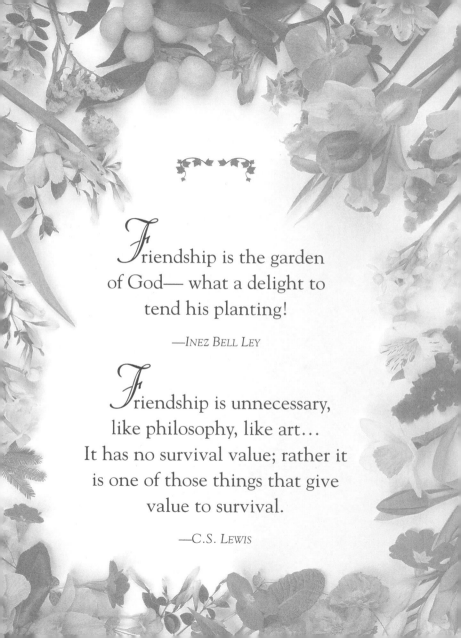

*F*riendship is the garden
of God— what a delight to
tend his planting!

—*INEZ BELL LEY*

*F*riendship is unnecessary,
like philosophy, like art…
It has no survival value; rather it
is one of those things that give
value to survival.

—*C.S. LEWIS*

A friend loves
at all times.

—PROVERBS 17:17

*T*here are veins in the hills where
jewels hide,
And gold lies buried deep;
There are harbor-towns
where the great ships ride,
And fame and fortune sleep;
But land and sea though we tireless rove,
And follow each trail to the end,
Whatever the wealth of our
treasure-trove, The best we shall find is
a friend.

—JOHN J. MOMENT

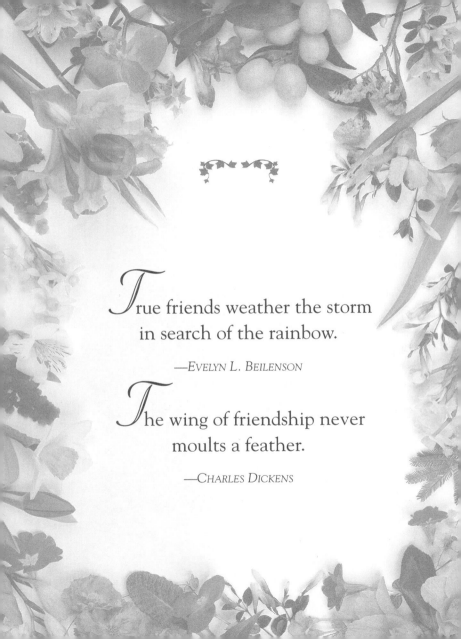

*T*rue friends weather the storm
in search of the rainbow.

—Evelyn L. Beilenson

*T*he wing of friendship never
moults a feather.

—Charles Dickens

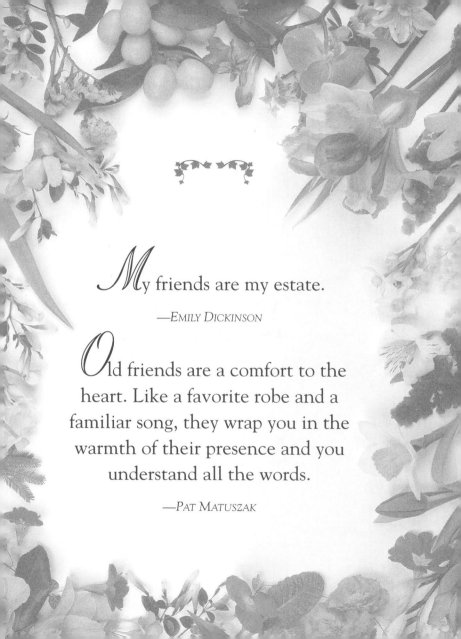

*M*y friends are my estate.

—Emily Dickinson

*O*ld friends are a comfort to the heart. Like a favorite robe and a familiar song, they wrap you in the warmth of their presence and you understand all the words.

—Pat Matuszak

I thank my
God every time
I remember you.

—PHILIPPIANS 1:3